Just the Facts

Terrorism

Richard Bingley

Heinemann
LIBRARY

www.heinemann.co.uk/library
Visit our website to find out more information about **Heinemann Library** books.

To order:

 Phone 44 (0) 1865 888066

 Send a fax to 44 (0) 1865 314091

 Visit the Heinemann Bookshop at www.heinemann.co.uk/library to browse our catalogue and order online.

Produced by Monkey Puzzle Media Ltd
Gissing's Farm, Fressingfield, Suffolk IP21 5SH, UK

First published in Great Britain by Heinemann Library, Halley Court, Jordan Hill, Oxford OX2 8EJ, part of Harcourt Education.
Heinemann is a registered trademark of Harcourt Education Ltd.

© Harcourt Education Ltd 2004
The moral right of the proprietor has been asserted.

Editorial: Sarah Eason and Georga Godwin
Design: Jamie Asher
Picture Research: Sally Cole
Consultant: Ian Derbyshire
Production: Edward Moore

Originated by Dot Gradations Ltd
Printed and bound in Hong Kong, China by
South China Printing Company

ISBN 0 431 16165 8
08 07 06 05 04
10 9 8 7 6 5 4 3 2 1

British Library Cataloguing in Publication Data
Bingley, Richard
Terrorism
303.6'25
A full catalogue record for this book is available from the British Library.

Acknowledgements
The publishers would like to thank the following for permission to reproduce photographs:
AKG p. **7**; Alamy pp. **30–31** (Felix Stensson), **49** (Paul Doyle); Associated Press pp. **4** (Suzanne Plunkett), **43** (Alessandro della Valle), **46** (Herve Merliac); Corbis pp. **9** (Bettmann), **24** (Roger Wood); Network Photographers pp. **19** (Mike Goldwater), **32** (Sion Touhia); Panos Pictures pp. **5** (Ami Vitale), **47** (J.C. Tordai); Press Association pp. **8**, **10** (EPA), **11** (John Giles), **13** (EPA), **14** (EPA), **15** (EPA), **17** (EPA), **18** (EPA), **20** (EPA), **21** (EPA), **22** (EPA), **25** (EPA), **26** (Johnny Green), **28** (EPA), **33** (EPA), **34** (EPA), **35**, **36** (Paul Faith), **37** (EPA), **39** (EPA), **40–41** (John Giles), **45** (EPA); Rex Features p. **50** (Sipa).

Cover photograph reproduced with permission of Rex Features (Tamara Beckwith).

Every effort has been made to contact copyright holders of any material reproduced in this book. Any omissions will be rectified in subsequent printings if notice is given to the publishers.

Any words appearing in the text in bold, **like this**, are explained in the Glossary.

Contents

What is terrorism?

The word 'terrorism' conjures up frightening images of human misery, with bombs exploding or aeroplanes full of terrified people being **hijacked**. Most people, most of the time, would agree that such acts of violence are as unacceptable as murder or armed robbery. So why do people often view terrorism differently from other violent crimes?

Incidents database

The University of St Andrews in Scotland runs the famous Centre for the Study of Terrorism and Political Violence, which keeps a database of serious terrorist incidents. Over 8000 have occurred since 1968. That's five attacks every week, with at least two involving the death of **civilians**.

There is an old saying: 'One person's terrorist is another's freedom fighter.' This means that while some might view an attack as 'terrorism', others may see the same act as the only way to promote what they believe is a just cause and force through the political changes they want to happen. Journalists and academics are often particularly keen not to take sides when describing a dispute. They sometimes use the softer term 'political violence' to describe terrorism.

New York office workers flee the collapsing World Trade Center, after it was struck by hijacked passenger jets on 11 September 2001.

Law-enforcement agencies such as the Central Intelligence Agency (CIA) in the USA work to understand terrorism, so it can be reduced or prevented. These agencies and other experts have established their own definitions of terrorism – all slightly different. A former CIA officer, Paul Pillar, says terrorism has four key elements. It is a violent act, or a serious threat of a violent act, that is:

1. planned beforehand
2. carried out to achieve political changes
3. aimed at civilians
4. usually the work of a group (not a country or army).

There are about 50 or 60 large terrorist groups in the world today. About half of these are inspired by religious differences. Other terrorist groups aim to bring about political changes, such as freedom from the rule of a foreign government. Some groups are motivated by single issues, such as trying to end research that involves using animals in tests.

Increased worldwide travel and modern technologies such as the Internet and mobile phones have made it easier for terrorists to carry out their plans. This is because it is harder for law-enforcement agencies (the police, military and other experts) to monitor their activities. The combination of new technologies and continued political and religious disputes means that terrorism is becoming more deadly and more widespread than ever before.

An activist from the Palestinian liberation group Hamas wields an automatic rifle in Gaza, in the Palestinian Authority.

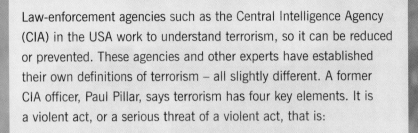

Terror before 1945

State terror

The word 'terrorism' was first used to describe events that
took place during the French Revolution (1789–99). In
1793, the last king of France, Louis XVI, was executed and
the **revolutionaries** took control of the government. They
introduced a brutal 'régime de la terreur' (reign of terror) to
strengthen their position. All those suspected of being
against the revolution were executed, mainly by guillotine.

The twentieth century saw further examples of terror inflicted
by governments. Joseph Stalin, leader of the **Soviet Union**
1924–53, and Adolf Hitler, leader of Nazi Germany
1933–45, massacred millions of victims who were opposed
to their government or who were viewed as 'undesirable'.

Political and religious terrorism

However, acts of terror inspired by political or religious
differences had been around for centuries. For example, in
India from the 7th century onwards, members of the
Thuggee **cult** strangled travellers as sacrifices to Kali, the
Hindu goddess of 'death and destruction'. The cult was
finally eradicated in the 19th century. In Persia (now Iran)
and Syria, from the 11th to the 13th century, members of a
secret organization of Muslim **fanatics** known as the
'Assassins' murdered many **Christian crusaders** who they
believed were enemies of their homelands and religion. They
operated from mountain fortresses and would sometimes
send secret agents to enemy camps and cities. They would
often plan their executions months in advance, and then
stab their victims in public. The words 'thug' and 'assassin'
have been associated with violence ever since.

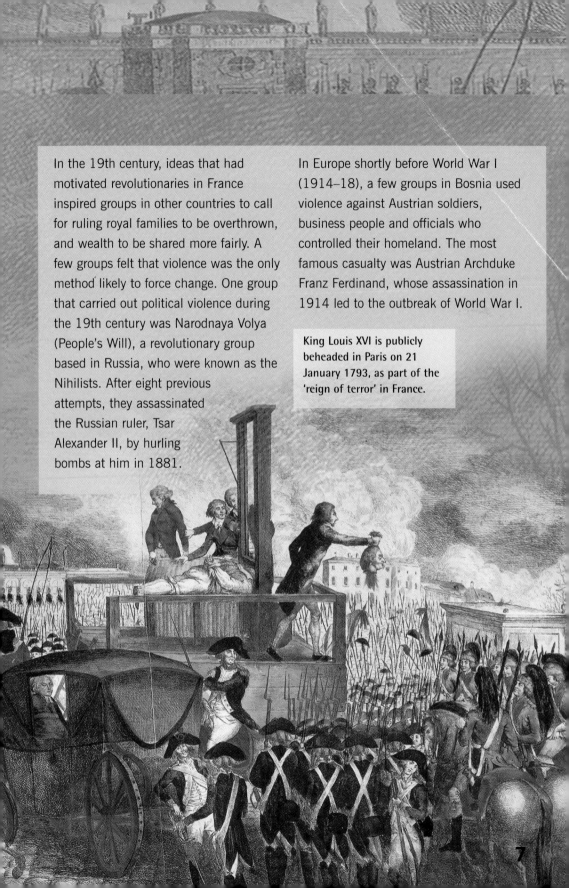

In the 19th century, ideas that had motivated revolutionaries in France inspired groups in other countries to call for ruling royal families to be overthrown, and wealth to be shared more fairly. A few groups felt that violence was the only method likely to force change. One group that carried out political violence during the 19th century was Narodnaya Volya (People's Will), a revolutionary group based in Russia, who were known as the Nihilists. After eight previous attempts, they assassinated the Russian ruler, Tsar Alexander II, by hurling bombs at him in 1881.

In Europe shortly before World War I (1914–18), a few groups in Bosnia used violence against Austrian soldiers, business people and officials who controlled their homeland. The most famous casualty was Austrian Archduke Franz Ferdinand, whose assassination in 1914 led to the outbreak of World War I.

King Louis XVI is publicly beheaded in Paris on 21 January 1793, as part of the 'reign of terror' in France.

Separatists and independence movements

Since 1945, terrorism has been understood as something committed by **non-state groups**, rather than governments. Many of these groups have been **separatists**, committed to freeing their land from being ruled or controlled by those they see as **occupying forces**.

After World War II (1939–45), **independence movements** in many countries tried to achieve freedom from their colonial rulers – countries such as Belgium, France and the UK that governed overseas territories (called colonies). In many parts of Asia, the **Middle East** and Africa, the occupying powers clung to power. In response, local armed groups formed to force their colonial rulers out. For example, in Algeria, North Africa, the National Liberation Front (FLN) wanted Algeria to be free from its French colonial rulers. During the late 1950s they shot and bombed French members of the public in a rebellion that caused the death of many Algerians too. Eventually France granted Algeria its independence in 1962.

In Northern Ireland the Provisional Irish Republican Army (Provisional IRA) used violence in its struggle to free Northern Ireland from British rule, and bring about the unification (joining) of Northern Ireland and southern Ireland (the Republic of Ireland). Some groups loyal to remaining as part of Britain (known as 'Loyalists') set up their own terrorism networks. So a cycle of violence remained in Northern Ireland, leading to over 3000 deaths in 30 years.

Masked Provisional IRA commandos.

Political causes

In the 1970s and 1980s most terror organizations were motivated by **left-wing** ideas and worked to spread **Marxist/socialist** revolution. The Red Brigades (Brigate Rosse), a left-wing group active in Italy during the 1970s and 1980s, committed a series of terrorist acts to bring attention to their ideas. In 1978 they kidnapped and murdered Aldo Moro, a former prime minister, before disbanding (breaking up) in 1984. In Germany, the Red Army Faction became Europe's most deadly urban terror group during the 1970s. They killed 30 to 50 people including German politicians, business people and US soldiers stationed in West Germany.

International terrorism

During this period, terrorism became an international problem, as activists operated increasingly beyond their own national boundaries. For example, in 1972, at the Olympic Games in Munich, Germany, eight Palestinian terrorists, from a group known as Black September, held nine Israeli athletes hostage. The activists believed this would draw attention to their cause – an end to what they saw as the occupation of their land by Jewish Israelis. All of the hostages and two other Israeli athletes were killed.

Munich Olympics siege, 1972: members of the Black September group take Israeli athletes hostage in front of a worldwide television audience.

...gious extremism

From the 1990s onwards the most deadly terror groups have been inspired by religious **extremism**. Some of this extremism, but not all, originates from the many unresolved disputes in the countries of the **Middle East**. These include the conflict between the Jewish Israelis and the mainly Muslim Palestinians (followers of the religion of Islam). **Islamic extremists** wage war here against the Jewish Israelis whom they see as the unjust occupiers of land once known as Palestine.

During the 1990s members of Islamic extremist groups such as Islamic Jihad and Al-Qaida began to spread around the world more than ever before. Their fighters travelled to many countries where there were conflicts involving Muslims, including Afghanistan, the Philippines, Bosnia and Algeria. These extremist groups also began to commit terrorist acts against Jews in Israel and against other countries in the **West** whose governments supported Israel. Examples include an attempt to destroy the World Trade Center in New York, USA in 1993 and the killing of 224 workers at US **embassies** in Kenya and Tanzania in Africa, in 1998.

Terrorism from Islamic extremists became much more internationally recognized after the terrorist attacks on US cities on 11 September 2001. A year later a nightclub in Bali, Indonesia, was bombed, killing 188 people, mostly Western tourists from Australia and Europe. A local group of Islamic extremists called Jemaa Islamiya was strongly suspected as responsible.

Guerrillas of the Revolutionary Armed Forces of Colombia (FARC) during a military parade in San Vicente, Colombia, 2001. The FARC are motivated by extreme left-wing political ideas (rather than religious extremism). Their activities include seizing land and natural resources which FARC claim only serve the interests of a few business people and corrupt Colombian politicians.

Political, ideological and separatist causes

By the mid-1990s, half of the better-known terrorist groups were supporting either political, **ideological** or **separatist** causes.

In South America, members of a group called the Revolutionary Armed Forces of Colombia (FARC) have used terrorism to promote their **left-wing** political and ideological aims. In Sri Lanka, Asia, a separatist group called the Tamil Tigers, which emerged in 1983, have used **suicide bombers** to force Sri Lanka's government to listen to their demands for a separate homeland in northern Sri Lanka for the Tamil people. Often these suicide bombers have been young women with explosives packed tight to their body, pretending to be pregnant.

In Northern Ireland, activists aiming to free Northern Ireland from British rule, continued to use terrorism to promote their cause. For example, in 1998, a car bomb killed 29 shoppers in the market town of Omagh, Northern Ireland. The bomb was placed by the small armed group known as the Real Irish Republican Army (Real IRA).

The funeral cortège of father and son victims of the 1998 Omagh market town bombing in Northern Ireland.

Methods

Funds

Background support for terrorism (training, equipment and travel, for example) costs millions of US dollars. Terrorists often fund their operations through bank robberies, kidnappings and ransoms, selling illegal drugs and counterfeiting money. Investigations have also shown that some international charities, businesses and banks have (often without knowing) directed money into the **Islamic extremist** organization Al-Qaida.

Organization

Terrorist groups are usually organized into small 'cells' (groups), with each cell having just a few members. These cells operate among millions of people – to locate them is like looking for a needle in a haystack. The members of these small groups often know very little about the activities of other cells. This means that, if captured, they are unable to reveal information about many of their colleagues.

Tactics, weapons and techniques

Terrorists use a variety of tactics. These include aircraft **hijackings**, mass shootings, assassinations, kidnappings and bombings. Bombs are sometimes delivered by cars or boats, or fired as missiles. Sometimes they are strapped to **suicide bombers** and sometimes they are detonated remotely.

The most common form of explosive is lawn fertilizer. Mixed with diesel fuel, just US$400 worth of this widely available product was used in the first major terrorist attack on New York's World Trade Center, in 1993. Six people were killed and a thousand were injured. The Islamic extremist Ramsi Yousef claimed responsibility and was jailed for life for the attacks.

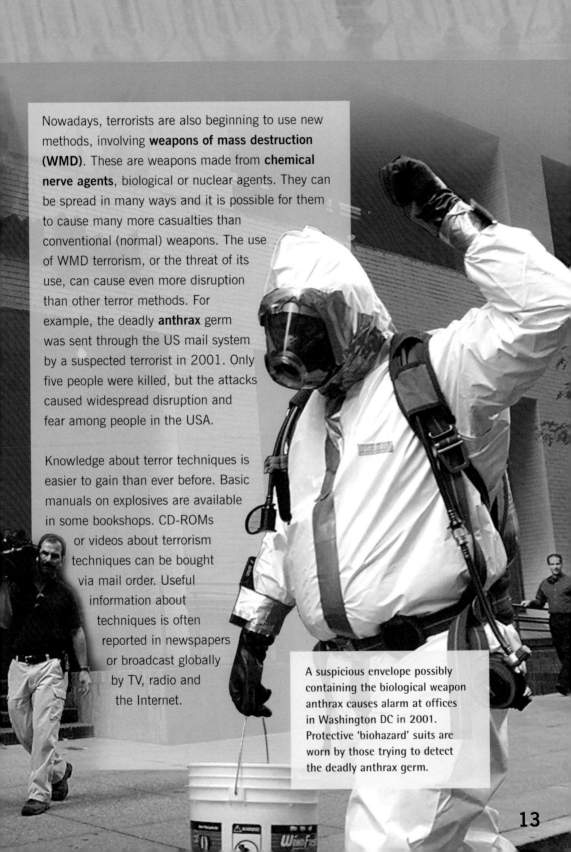

Nowadays, terrorists are also beginning to use new methods, involving **weapons of mass destruction (WMD)**. These are weapons made from **chemical nerve agents**, biological or nuclear agents. They can be spread in many ways and it is possible for them to cause many more casualties than conventional (normal) weapons. The use of WMD terrorism, or the threat of its use, can cause even more disruption than other terror methods. For example, the deadly **anthrax** germ was sent through the US mail system by a suspected terrorist in 2001. Only five people were killed, but the attacks caused widespread disruption and fear among people in the USA.

Knowledge about terror techniques is easier to gain than ever before. Basic manuals on explosives are available in some bookshops. CD-ROMs or videos about terrorism techniques can be bought via mail order. Useful information about techniques is often reported in newspapers or broadcast globally by TV, radio and the Internet.

A suspicious envelope possibly containing the biological weapon anthrax causes alarm at offices in Washington DC in 2001. Protective 'biohazard' suits are worn by those trying to detect the deadly anthrax germ.

13

Motives for terrorism

Most people who commit acts of terror would not accept that they are terrorists. They feel guided by a higher cause, and think the use of extreme violence – even against members of the public – is necessary if they are to achieve their aims. Each terror organization has a slightly different set of aims, but most are loosely inspired by one of four motives: religious **extremism**, **separatism**, **political idealism**, or a belief in a single issue.

Religious extremism

For some members of extreme religious groups, violence against non-believers becomes a divine duty. This means they feel that their god would expect them to defend their religion by attacking those who are members of a different religion or who are non-believers. They do not worry about losing public and political support, because they believe their god is always on their side. Their terrorism is based less on practical victories like changing laws, and more upon generally destroying the enemy.

Some religious extremists believe that followers who die or commit suicide during an attack will move on to paradise as a reward for their actions. They are worshipped as **martyrs**.

Eighty people are killed in a Moscow bomb blast in September 1999; Russian authorities blame terrorists from Chechnya in southern Russia.

Separatism

Many terrorist groups have stated that their goal is to be free from being ruled by those who they believe are unjustly occupying their land. Violent groups seeking to free themselves from a foreign occupier do not see themselves as terrorists. They prefer to be seen as 'freedom fighters' and refer to their goal as national **liberation.** 'Freedom fighters' have recently committed terrorist acts in Northern Ireland (Provisional IRA and Real IRA), Spain (Euskadi ta Askatasuna, ETA), Sri Lanka (Tamil Tigers), Russia (Chechen separatists), Israel (Hamas and Islamic Jihad) and Turkey (Kurdistan Workers Party, PKK).

Political idealism and single issues

Sometimes those with extreme **left-wing** or **right-wing** political views or those wishing to promote a single issue such as animal rights are driven to commit acts of terrorism. They believe that violence is the only way to make the wider community or those in authority listen to their views. They believe that otherwise they would be ignored.

Grosny, Chechnya's capital city, is bombed by Russia's air force in October 1999 in response to attacks blamed on Chechen fighters.

Extremist religious groups

From the 1980s the number of terrorist incidents motivated by religious **extremism** has increased greatly. Some of this terrorism has been inspired by **Islamic extremism**, but people claiming to be motivated by other religions have also committed acts of terrorism.

In the 1990s the Japanese Aum Shinrikyo (Supreme Truth) **cult**, led by the mysterious Shoko Asahara, tried to buy weapons-grade plutonium, a material used to make nuclear bombs. In March 1995 Shoko's followers sprayed poisonous gas around Tokyo's subway system. Twelve people were killed and 5000 injured.

In April 1995, furious at the spread of government rules in the USA, Timothy McVeigh blew up federal (central government) offices in Oklahoma City, killing 168 people. He was inspired by extreme **right-wing** Christian religious groups. Like Islamic extremist groups, these groups had local hatreds and concerns within US society. They also inspired hatred of non-Christians, especially Jews and non-white people. In the same year, Israel's Prime Minister Yitzhak Rabin was assassinated by Yigal Amir, a Jewish **fanatic**. Amir opposed the Prime Minister's attempts to make peace with the mainly Muslim Palestinians and told police he had acted on the 'orders of God'.

The spread of Islamic terrorism is partly due to the continued conflict between Jewish-controlled Israel and the mainly Muslim Palestinians who live in the same territory. The armed Palestinian groups, Hamas (Zeal) and Islamic Jihad, wage a 'holy war' (jihad) against Israel. They see the **'liberation** of all of Palestine' from Israel as a religious duty and **suicide bombers** are worshipped as **martyrs**. In response, Israeli governments have seized Palestinian land and attacked Palestinian towns. Both sides claim to be defending themselves and accuse the other side of terrorism. As a result, many Israeli and Palestinian **civilians** have been killed.

Al-Qaida, the most famous Islamic extremist terror group, has taken the 'holy war' beyond the **Middle East**. It has declared a death sentence upon the USA, its friends in Europe (for their support of Israel) and the Muslim countries that have close relations with the USA, such as Saudi Arabia.

Suicide-bomb candidates belonging to the group Hamas hold the Koran holy book next to their explosives belts in South Lebanon, 2002.

Al-Qaida

Al-Qaida (The Base) originated from armed resistance groups in Afghanistan, a mainly Muslim country. Mujaheddin (Muslim holy warriors) fighters resisted and eventually defeated **Soviet Union** troops that occupied Afghanistan during the 1980s. After the Soviet troops had withdrawn from Afghanistan, one of the leaders of the Mujaheddin, a Saudi Arabian called Osama bin Laden, turned his attention to other struggles that he believed threatened Muslims. With the Palestinian religious scholar Abdullah Azzam, he recruited and trained fighters and terror groups, forming a new network called Al-Qaida.

Al-Qaida's main aim is to spread Sharia (strict Islamic) law. It set up home in Afghanistan, where it was offered refuge by the strict Islamic Talibaan government. From here it trained around 100,000 fighters in religious and military teachings. It sent its followers around the world and formed networks with existing **Islamic extremist** groups in other countries.

Gradually bin Laden's group turned on the USA. In bin Laden's eyes, the USA was trying to destroy the Islamic religion by stationing troops in Saudi Arabia near Mecca (the home city of Islam), and arming the Jewish state of Israel, built on old Palestinian (mainly Muslim) land. Bin Laden regularly referred to the USA as 'the great Satan', and destroying the USA became a holy cause for Al-Qaida. In 1998 bin Laden issued a death sentence against the USA, her allies and Israel.
In 1998 car bombs killed 224 and injured around 5000 people at US **embassies** in Kenya and Tanzania.

Osama bin Laden is head of the modern world's most dangerous terrorist organization, known as Al-Qaida.

In September 2001 over 3000 people lost their lives in the USA as **hijacked** planes destroyed the World Trade Center in New York and crashed into the Pentagon building in Washington. Although Al-Qaida never claimed responsibility for these attacks, much evidence came to light that made them prime suspects.

Terrifying features of these attacks were that the attackers set out to kill as many people as possible and were totally unconcerned about public opinion. And no prior warning was given beforehand to limit the number of casualties or identify the attackers.

Al-Qaida has recruited commandos from 40 nationalities. Evidence from seized computers, court cases and their training camps in Afghanistan shows Al-Qaida has become the first terror group with a truly worldwide reach.

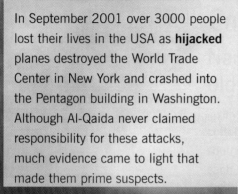

Islamic holy warriors (Mujaheddin) guard the approach to Kabul, Afghanistan by lighting flares at the Bala Hisar Fort.

❝Al-Qaida has a head start of ten years, so the fight has just begun.❞

Terrorism expert Dr Rohan Gunaratna, 27 June 2002, Columbia International Affairs On-line

11 September 2001

The 11 September 2001 terrorist attacks were the world's worst ever terrorism disaster and they sent shock waves throughout the world. The simplicity of the terrorists' methods, and the fact they were caught by live television coverage, meant much of the world was asking who might be targeted next?

By first training as pilots at flight schools and smuggling knives aboard four passenger jets, terrorists were able to seize control of aeroplanes across the USA. Over New York, the first passenger jet was deliberately flown into the North Tower of the World Trade Center by five suicide-**hijackers**. Twenty minutes later, a second jet seized by another five hijackers flew into the Trade Center's South Tower. Shortly after, both towers collapsed while office workers tried to escape and emergency services were helping them.

Thirty minutes later near Washington DC a third passenger plane flew into the giant Pentagon building, home to the US Department of Defense. One hundred and eighty-nine people died, including all those who were on board the jet.

The World Trade Center in New York begins to collapse after each tower is struck by a hijacked passenger jet.

❝There are good causes and bad causes. But there is no such thing as a good terrorist.❞

US President George W. Bush after the 11 September 2001 attacks

A firefighter looks down on to the debris of the destroyed World Trade Center where around 3000 people died on 11 September 2001.

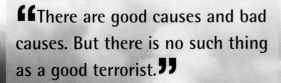

Another hijacked jet crashed 30 minutes later in Pennsylvania, killing all 45 passengers. The US State Department said that the intended target of the fourth plane was 'not known'. They believe passengers overpowered the four hijackers, preventing the plane from being used as a guided 'missile' to hit buildings and kill many more people. In total the hijackers caused the deaths of over 3000 people. Victims of the Trade Center attacks alone came from 78 countries. All nineteen hijackers died in the attacks and can never be questioned. They have been linked by evidence to Al-Qaida's network. Suspects had prepared for their operations in Europe and learnt to fly in the USA.

After the attack of 11 September, countries understood that they would have to work together to combat future terrorism. Indeed, many felt that if they had worked better together before 11 September, the attacks could have been prevented. Because of this feeling, strong **counter-terrorism** actions followed.

Separatist groups

The aims of **separatist** groups vary, depending on different local circumstances. Some groups aim to expel a foreign occupier from their land and achieve outright national independence. Others demand that their own culture be respected. For example, they may want their own language to be taught or used in schools.

Independence movements continue to exist where disputes about the control and ownership of land remain unresolved. The Provisional IRA has tried to force the British government to give up its control of Northern Ireland for over 30 years. Tamil Tigers fight against Sri Lanka's government for regional independence on the island. The Kurdish PKK seeks a separate nation for **ethnic** Kurds living in Turkey.

Some groups have now declared **ceasefires** after 30 years of armed struggle. The Provisional IRA and its Loyalist enemies in Northern Ireland, the PKK in Turkey and the Tamil Tigers in Sri Lanka have all tied themselves (some say temporarily) to pursuing their goals through peaceful politics. ETA, a group committed to establishing a nation state for ethnic Basques living in France and Spain, remain actively bombing and shooting their opponents, or those simply caught in the crossfire. ETA have killed over 800 people since taking up arms in 1968.

Russia has faced an armed separatist uprising by Muslim **guerrillas** in the mountainous southern republic of Chechnya since the early 1990s. The struggle has claimed the lives of tens of thousands of Russians and Chechens. Since 1999 Chechen terrorists have been connected to bomb attacks on Russian cities, including Moscow, and links with the **Islamic extremist** Al-Qaida network are claimed by Russia.

An underground car park in Santander, northern Spain, is bombed by the Basque terrorist group ETA in December 2002.

The most violent example is in the Jewish state of Israel, which Palestinians believe was built on Palestinian land. Between September 2000 and January 2003, over 650 Israeli citizens were murdered by **suicide bombers** supporting the Palestinians in their aim to achieve a separate, independent state for Palestine. During the same period around 1500 Palestinians were killed by Israeli forces. Although this conflict is about the political idea of a separate state for the Palestinians, it is fuelled by the religious tension between Jews and Muslims.

23

Political or ideological groups

Some terrorism is carried out to bring attention to a set of political ideas. These are ideas about how human beings should organize and run their society. Some groups with **left-wing**, **Marxist/socialist** and anti-**Western** beliefs have been ruthless in pursuit of their causes.

In Peru, South America, the Shining Path (Sendero Luminoso) started out with left-wing ideals, aiming for a peasant-based revolution. Yet it has bombed, shot and kidnapped government opponents and innocent people since the 1980s. Over 30,000 people have been killed, either by direct terrorism or by being caught in the middle of conflict between government forces and the Shining Path's army of 2500 **guerrillas**.

The Japanese Red Army (JRA) seeks worldwide Marxist revolution and to overthrow the Japanese emperor. But curiously it is based thousands of miles away in Bekaa Valley, Lebanon – home to many terrorism groups. The JRA's most lethal attack was at Israel's Lod Airport in 1972. They bombed and shot dead 26 **civilians**, injuring 80. Like the Shining Path in Peru, the JRA's aims have become unclear – attacking anybody who crosses their path. Its last famous activity was being hired by Libya's leader, Colonel Khadafi, to attack US targets at the end of the 1980s.

Bekaa Valley in Lebanon is a major wine-producing region, but has also been home to many international terror groups.

In Greece, a left-wing group called 'November 17' have claimed responsibility for 21 murders, including those of Greek, US and UK officials and business persons. The group is named after a famous student demonstration against the Greek dictatorship government on 17 November 1973. It is thought to be an extremely small group, with around 25 members. It had avoided capture for almost 30 years, but its suspected leaders were finally arrested in 2002.

However, terrorists motivated by political ideas have usually been more restrained and less lethal than those inspired by religious **extremism**. They are aware that too much violence might turn people against their cause.

'Feliciano', leader of Red Path, part of the Shining Path movement salutes defiantly as he is captured in 1999 after a four-year man hunt in Peru.

Single-issue terrorist groups

Single-issue terrorist groups are those that turn to violence to promote a single cause, such as saving the natural environment, animal rights or stopping abortions. Some groups use terror tactics to gain publicity for their cause, believing that violence is necessary if they are to achieve their aims.

Activists who carry out 'eco-terrorism' claim to be concerned about the destruction of the natural environment, especially by big corporations. For eighteen years, Theodore Kaczynski, known as the 'unabomber', acted alone in mailing bombs to universities and airlines. Three victims were killed and 29 left injured. He criticized technology and the destruction of the environment, declaring that he would stop bombing if his manifesto (set of aims) was published by journalists.

Animal rights **extremists** have turned to attacking laboratories where animal research takes place and also on scientists who carry out experiments on animals. In the UK, during the winter of 2000/01 a mail bomber sent fifteen letter bombs, which left a child scarred for life and a woman without her left eye. Attacks are sometimes carried out in the name of an international network with no apparent leader, called the Animal Liberation Front.

Anti-abortion campaigners often call themselves 'pro-life' activists. A tiny number of these activists turn to terrorism. They target doctors and clinics involved in abortion services. In 1997, pro-life terrorists bombed a clinic in Birmingham, USA, killing a security guard. In 1998, a doctor was shot dead by a sniper at his home in Buffalo, USA. According to the USA-based campaign group the National Organization for Women (NOW), eight people have been murdered and sixteen wounded by anti-abortion terrorism in North America alone. Anti-abortionist terrorists sometimes have links with extreme Christian groups. They also share some of the features of other religious terrorism groups, such as extreme intolerance of other people's beliefs and lifestyles.

Some single-issue activists claim that they are not violent against animals or humans, and say that they just destroy property, which they see as vandalism rather than terrorism. Others use 'fear tactics' such as making menacing telephone calls or threatening to bomb homes and workplaces. Spreading fear and panic rather than carrying out violent action is classified as terrorism by many law-enforcement agencies. Such incidents generate extreme terror for political ends.

Those who feel strongly about single issues rarely turn to terrorism. In contrast to the Animal liberation front, non-violent groups such as the People for Ethical Treatment of Animals (PETA) use direct action and media stunts to draw attention to their campaign for animal rights.

Terrorism in the future

Experts believe that terrorist activities will cause an increasing number of casualties in the future. This is partly because many more are motivated by religious **extremism** and those who commit them are more **fanatical**. Also, technology is now available that will allow more devastating and murderous attacks.

Weapons of mass destruction

Many fear that terrorists will use **weapons of mass destruction (WMD)** to take revenge against their enemies or when promoting a cause. WMD are nuclear, chemical or **biological weapons** that can have a far more devastating impact than conventional weapons.

A nuclear bomb explosion would kill many thousands of people and leave an area poisoned for several years. Many, but not all, experts feel that it is unlikely that a **non-state group** would be able to develop nuclear bombs. They cost millions (if not billions) of dollars to develop and they are extremely dangerous to handle and transport. They also demand much time and skill to produce.

Passengers await medical help in Tokyo, Japan, after the Aum Shinrikyo cult sprayed nerve gas in a subway station in 1995.

Nuclear terrorism is therefore likely to come in two other forms. Firstly, normal explosives like nitro-glycerine or TNT could be mixed with nuclear materials. Such a mix would increase the power of an explosion and temporarily leave an area polluted by **radioactivity**. This kind of bomb is known as a 'dirty bomb'. Secondly, evidence suggests that some terrorists have looked into attacking nuclear power plants either by rocket-propelled missiles or by flying into them with aeroplanes. This could cause a massive initial explosion. Afterwards a harmful radioactive cloud might spread, contaminating hundreds of miles of the surrounding environment.

WMD have already been used in terrorism, firstly by the Japanese cult, Aum Shinrikyo. Inspired by their leader, Shoko Asahara, supporters of the cult killed 12 and injured 5000 people in a Tokyo subway station in 1995 by spraying sarin gas – a **chemical nerve agent** that causes sickness, paralysis and choking. Aum Shinrikyo had already unsuccessfully attempted to use the deadly biological toxins (poisons), botulinum and **anthrax**. Later, in the USA, five people died from anthrax infection after deadly spores were posted to politicians and journalists. These biological weapons, sent just after the 11 September 2001 attacks, caused widespread panic and fear, and demonstrated the social disruption terrorists are able to create.

Terrorism in the future

Agro-terrorism

Agro-terrorism is the use of biological weapons or chemical nerve agents to poison crops or livestock in an attempt to disrupt the human food supply. Terrorist attacks upon agriculture could destroy many crops. They could also lead to the slaughter of millions of farm animals if the animals were deliberately infected with diseases. In the 1980s Tamil extremists in Sri Lanka threatened to infect rubber trees with leaf curl and to poison tea-crops. It is thought the plot was never carried out, but many experts classify serious threats such as this as terrorism.

The Itaipu Dam on the Brazil/Paraguay border is almost five miles long and home to the world's largest hydroelectric power plant. By seizing control of the computers that control dam floodgates, cyber-terrorists could cause widespread devastation.

Cyber-terrorism

Computer networks are also targets for terrorist groups. Disruptive attacks against computer systems are known as 'cyber-terrorism'.

Computers now run vast systems that control communications, energy, money, transport, health and emergency services. Tapping into them and disrupting them from cyberspace (via the Internet) could have catastrophic consequences. For example, by using the Internet terrorists might be able to seize control of the computers that control dam floodgates or power stations. By doing so they could kill many people, destroy vast areas or land, or hold a government to ransom. If the politicians did not grant the terrorists' demands, then huge devastation might follow.

In Russia, in 2000, the Interior Ministry revealed that the country's gas supplier Gazprom temporarily lost control of the central switchboard that controls gas flows in the pipeline. Computer **hackers** had taken over control of the switchboard. In 1998 **ethnic** Tamil **guerrillas**, calling themselves 'Internet Black Tigers', sent 800 menacing and disruptive emails a day over a period of two weeks to **embassies** in Sri Lanka. Like other forms of terrorism, cyber-terrorism does not necessarily involve lethal attacks. Its aim may be to create as much disruption and panic as possible.

Cyber-activists have also used the Internet to make public the names of staff at abortion clinics and animal-testing centres. By advertising addresses and telephone numbers, they have given more hardened activists an opportunity to threaten and attack staff.

No known cyberspace attack has so far killed people, but such attacks are being reported more regularly. Experts are especially concerned about terrorist bombs filled with weapons of mass destruction exploding at the same time as 'hacktivists' disable the computers of emergency services, such as ambulances and fire brigades.

Terrorist arguments

Terrorists sometimes attempt to justify their actions by saying that if they did not commit acts of violence their cause would be ignored by politicians. The Black September group, an armed wing of the **Palestinian Liberation Organization (PLO)**, kidnapped and killed nine Israeli athletes at the 1972 Munich Olympics. It is thought that a quarter of the world followed the events as they were broadcast via the television and radio. Soon afterwards, Yasser Arafat, the leader of the PLO, was invited to address the **United Nations** (UN). The PLO's cause, a separate state for Palestinians, ignored for many years, was now gaining powerful worldwide attention.

Some groups claim to take up violence reluctantly, only after all other non-violent actions such as protests and political talks have failed. They say that they are responding to threats, perhaps from a foreign occupier, brutal political leaders, or opposing forces which threaten the destruction of their own religion. They call themselves 'freedom fighters' and 'defenders' rather than 'terrorists'.

Many activists say that they commit acts of violence because of the harsh treatment they receive from those who are ruling over them. Some people in some countries are kept in absolute poverty by their governments, and some people live in fear of military attack. In these situations people can become desperate, and aggressive responses become more likely.

Young Palestinians throw stones at Israel's army in the West Bank town of Ramallah, in the Palestinian Authority, April 1997.

Some activists have eventually won power. From 1948–94, South Africa was governed by the minority white population who practised a system of apartheid (separateness). Black people were denied the right to vote in elections and there were laws that banned black and white people from mixing. The black population were left to live in terrible poverty, given the worst property, land and jobs. Nelson Mandela was leader of 'Spear of the Nation'. This was the armed wing of the African National Congress (ANC), a political group committed to running a **democratic**, non-racial, South Africa.

In 1964 Nelson Mandela was branded a terrorist and imprisoned by the South African government. In 1990, after massive national and international support, he was released. He was elected South Africa's president in 1994. Nowadays most people accept that Mandela was a 'freedom fighter' trying to overthrow the unfair system of apartheid.

❝It [terrorism] achieves publicity for the cause terrorists are supporting.❞

Dame Stella Rimington, former head of UK intelligence agency MI5, the Guardian, 4 September 2002

Nelson Mandela, head of the once-outlawed ANC political party, swears an oath of office as he is made President of South Africa in 1994.

33

Arguments against terrorism

The reality of terrorism is that it is horrifying and cruel, ruining the lives of many innocent victims and their families. People have the right to life and to live free from violence and fear. Many people and groups are in desperate situations but don't turn to terrorism.

Terrorism is unfair and undemocratic. Victims of terrorist attacks are often killed because of things they cannot help, such as their nationality. Or it may be that the victims were simply in the wrong place at the wrong time. Terrorists are also punishing victims for not sharing their own views. By deciding that their own ambitions and views are much more important than the ambitions or views of a victim they are saying that they are more significant than other people.

Basque communities take to the streets to protest against the terrorism carried out by violent ETA activists in Spain.

Those carrying out terrorism on behalf of a particular community or idea often spoil the reputation of an entire group of people or cause. There are other dramatic methods of drawing attention to a cause. For example, in the 1970s and 1980s, imprisoned political activists who wanted Ireland to be united and free from British rule (Irish Republicans) went on **hunger strikes**. Ten starved themselves to death in 1981–82. These hunger strikes caused many more people to sympathize with the Irish Republicans' cause than brutal terror tactics ever did.

In many places, such as Colombia and Sri Lanka, terrorism has led to civil war. This harms the lives of the very people the terrorists claim to defend. If a government decides to crack down strongly upon terrorist networks, thousands of innocent people may be killed. Terrorists can hardly be praised for 'defending' their communities if this occurs.

There are reasons why the people of a country should not be held responsible for the actions of their government, even in a democratic state. One is that people may have voted against the political party in government, but it still wins power. Another is that the major political parties sometimes offer no different choice of policy. So voters often cannot change the actions of their government, even if they want to.

❝Hunger strikes were better recruiters than bomb-strikes.❞

Professor Michael Kearney, talking about the Provisional IRA's 30-year terrorism campaign to unite Ireland

Provisional IRA activist Bobby Sands, who died 5 May 1981, aged 27, in a Belfast prison after 65 days of a hunger strike.

Terrorism and the law

In any civilized society people have a right to live free from fear and violence. Terrorism uses violence to achieve its aims, and cannot be tolerated – it is therefore made illegal in countries around the world. People committing acts of terrorism are charged as criminals, tried in a courtroom and sent to prison. Yet because each case of terrorism is different, governments have difficulty in drawing up one set of clear laws to cover the many unique terrorism situations.

Sometimes anti-terrorism laws can seem harsh. In some countries where terrorism is frequent, 'internment' is used. This is where suspected terrorists are held in prison without trial – for the safety of the wider population. The UK used internment to combat terrorism by Irish terrorist groups such as the Provisional IRA. However, it stopped when the Provisional IRA declared a **ceasefire** in the 1990s. Following the attacks of 11 September 2001, a softer form of internment was introduced in the UK. The Anti-Terrorism Act 2001 says potentially dangerous individuals can be held without trial, but are free to go back to their home country if they are foreign nationals.

Sometimes the victims of terrorism and those living in communities that suffer political violence think that the laws against terrorism are too soft. During the peace processes in Ireland and Israel during the 1990s, some terror groups agreed to give up arms if other members of their groups were released from jail. Armed activists said that they should be viewed as 'political prisoners' and released like 'prisoners of war', because the armed struggle had ended. Many in these countries felt distress when people who had murdered and injured people from their communities were released from jail early.

The Maze Prison near Lisburn, Northern Ireland. Terrorists and suspects were housed in blocks of cells shaped like the letter 'H'.

State-sponsored terrorism

Some governments around the world have been accused of giving support, in the form of money, arms and training, to terrorist groups abroad. This problem has become known as 'state-sponsored terrorism'. In Iran, after the revolution in 1979, Ayatollah Khomeini became the country's leader. He was a radical Muslim and was angered by what he saw as Israel taking land from Palestinian Muslims. His government helped arm and train violent groups such as Hizbullah and Islamic Jihad to make attacks against Israel. They sometimes targeted Israel's **Western** friends, such as the USA. During the 1980s, Libya's leader, Colonel Khadhafi, sent arms and trained Irish terrorists, including members of the Provisional IRA.

'Camp X-Ray' at the USA's Guantánamo Bay Naval Base, Cuba, holds Talibaan and Al-Qaida suspects captured in the US-led war in Afghanistan in 2001.

National counter-terrorism

Counter-terrorism means steps taken by law-enforcement agencies (the police, military and other experts) to prevent and tackle terrorism. By better understanding terrorism they improve chances of stopping further attacks.

Identifying terrorists is often compared to 'searching for a needle in a haystack'. This is not just because so few of the Earth's 6.5 billion inhabitants are terrorists. Other complications also arise. For example, long before terrorists first bombed New York's World Trade Center in 1993, city police received a daily average of ten hoax telephone calls from self-confessed bombers. Crank telephone calls were part of their average working day. It is extremely difficult for the police to decide which calls to take seriously. And there are not enough police to investigate them all.

Although it is the police who arrest and charge terrorists, they are usually acting on information from 'intelligence agencies'. These agencies secretly investigate threats to national security. Famous examples include the Federal Bureau of Investigation (FBI) and Central Intelligence Agency (CIA) in the USA, MI5 (home security) and MI6 (security abroad) in the UK, and the Australian Secret Intelligence Service (ASIS) in Australia.

Sometimes agencies secretly 'place' a person into a suspicious group to spy on their activities and report back. This is known as infiltration. Agencies also monitor emails and telephone calls of suspected terrorists. Various Witness Protection Programmes operate in countries keen to get information from ex-terrorists. These offer activists a change of identity and a guarantee of safety if they leave a violent group and give information about the group's activities.

The USA in particular takes counter-terrorism very seriously. It aims to spend US$30 billion every year on counter-terrorism and formed a Department for Homeland Security following the attacks on 11 September 2001.

Effective counter-terrorism measures virtually closed down groups like the Red Army Faction in Germany in the 1980s. During the 1980s and 1990s, weapons supplies to Irish terrorist groups from the Czech Republic and Libya were also stopped. Just as terrorism advances with technology, so counter-terrorism measures improve too.

Logan Airport in Boston, Mass., USA, is reopened after the 11 September 2001 terrorism attacks on the World Trade Center. Security is intensified across the USA.

"Fighting terrorism is like being a goalkeeper. You can make a hundred brilliant saves but the only shot that people remember is the one that gets past you."

Professor Paul Wilkinson, University of St Andrews, Scotland

International counter-terrorism

The Internet, mobile telephones, international finance, unrestricted travel and the availability of terrible weapons now make terrorism an international problem. Therefore, countries need to cooperate more and adopt international **counter-terrorism** measures to tackle violent extremists who travel the world.

The USA tried for many years to use financial and **diplomatic** force against states which it said offered 'support' to terrorists. After the deaths of so many people following 11 September 2001, its patience snapped. With the help of 55 countries, US-led armies removed the Talibaan government in Afghanistan. The USA believed the Talibaan had been supporting the terrorist group Al-Qaida, which it held responsible for terrorist attacks on 11 September.

What the US government described as the 'global coalition against terror' in 2001 (also known more simply as the 'war on terrorism') is not confined to Afghanistan. Military training and arms have been given by the USA to the governments of Yemen, Georgia and the Philippines to crack down on people suspected of operating on behalf of Al-Qaida in those countries. However, some people worry that some governments with poor human rights records could use US training and weapons to crack down viciously on any of their opponents, not just terrorists.

Menwith Hill US military base in Yorkshire, UK, which can monitor satellite communications across the world.

National police agencies exchange information with other countries through an organization called Interpol (International Criminal Police Organization). Based in France, Interpol has 179 member countries. All send in information relating to terrorist incidents, which is then shared among members. Also, countries that have long-standing friendships with one another share secret information. Australia, Canada, New Zealand, the UK and USA run the Echelon system. This uses space satellites and land-based domes, shaped like giant golf balls, to scoop up information from millions of faxes, emails and telephones. Echelon is programmed to identify individual voices and important words and names in the hunt for terrorists.

The European Union (EU) has also been active in combating terrorism. In December 2001 the EU officially named 42 terrorist people and groups who threaten peace in Europe. Some months later the EU and USA began working jointly on blocking money supplies from their own countries to groups they say have terrorist links.

The United Nations

The United Nations (UN) is an international organization set up by countries to work together to achieve international peace and security. Most of the world's countries are now members of the UN.

The UN's most important governing document is the Universal Declaration of Human Rights. Article Three of this document says: 'Everyone has the right to life, liberty and security.' The UN believes that human beings should never be subjected to the cruelty terrorism brings, no matter how convincing the terrorists' cause might be.

The UN is sometimes known as the 'international community'. It manages agencies around the world promoting safety in their special field. For example, the International Atomic Energy Agency guards against nuclear materials falling into dangerous hands. The International Civil Aviation Organization looks into ways to guard aeroplanes from **hijackers** and bombs.

The UN has also passed many conventions (agreements). Member countries try to prevent terrorism through sharing information so terrorists are stopped and brought to justice. In 1999 a convention for the 'Suppression of terrorist bombing' set up a UN Terrorism Prevention Branch. States are also now held more responsible for their own residents who might be plotting terrorism abroad. The 'Charter of the UN' grants powers to punish through **diplomacy** or trade (such as stopping aircraft flights), and finally armed force, those that threaten and sponsor 'breaches of the peace'.

The United Nations headquarters, based in New York, USA.

UN **counter-terrorism** work also includes stopping the supply of money to terrorist organizations. This is done by encouraging teamwork between financial bodies, such as international banks and law-enforcement agencies, such as the police. The biggest terrorism-prevention agency is the US Foreign Terrorist Asset Tracking Center. According to the US Defense Secretary Donald Rumsfeld, those in 'bankers pinstripes' rather than military uniforms will find and stop terrorists.

There are disagreements between UN members about who or which groups should be called 'terrorists'. The UN is therefore still unable to create one final definition of terrorism. However, because most member states have been victims of terrorism, and are worried about the future, a 1999 UN resolution (formal agreement) 'strongly condemns all acts, methods and practices of terrorism as criminal and unjustifiable, wherever and by whomever committed'.

❝Each [terrorist atrocity] is a reminder that terrorism is a uniquely barbaric and cowardly crime.❞

UK Prime Minister Tony Blair addressing the UN General Assembly, 21 September 1998

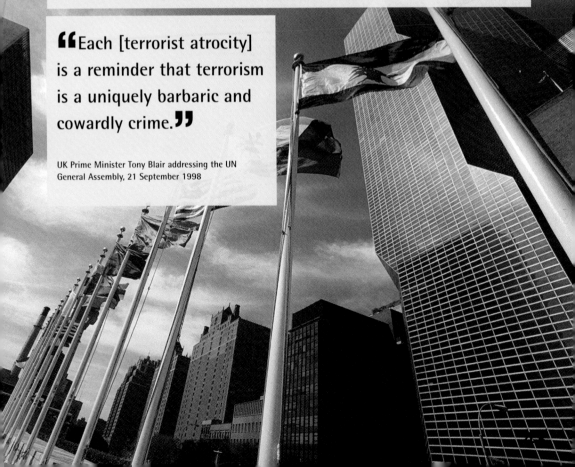

Coping with terrorism

Terrorism is deliberately used to spread fear among members of the public, and increasingly members of the public are targets themselves. Terrorism does not just cause dreadful physical wounds to those at the scene, but creates lasting damage to victims, governments and sometimes entire populations.

For every person tragically killed by terrorism there are usually many injured. Those who escape with their lives are often left disabled. After a terrorist incident, most victims suffer from trauma (severe emotional shock). Sometimes this emotional suffering lasts for the rest of their lives. Sufferers are not always those at the scene, but may be close family members, friends or even those who witnessed brutal terrorism inflicted upon others. Some victims cannot stop thinking about the incident and may have nightmares, or become afraid to leave their homes. Some grieve at the loss of loved ones, and even feel guilty and angry about surviving. Most of all a sense of helplessness can occur, with the feeling of control over one's own life shattered.

There are also consequences for a wider society that experiences terrorism. Tourists and business people may stop travelling and trading in areas, because their safety is threatened. This can lead to loss of money and livelihoods. People can become less tolerant and more suspicious. For example, after it was reported that a small group of Arab-Muslims might be responsible for the attacks upon US cities in September 2001, some air travellers refused to board aeroplanes alongside Arab passengers.

Increased suspicion can limit all of our freedoms. For example, checks at airports might take much longer, or in extreme circumstances curfews are put on communities to stop people leaving their houses at set times.

An American flag is flown by emergency service workers searching for bodies among the rubble of the destroyed World Trade Center two weeks after the attacks in 2001.

In their efforts to cope with terrorism, some governments clamp down viciously upon terrorists, or anybody under suspicion. In doing so they may commit **human rights abuses**. This can drive people to join the terrorists' cause and acts of terrorism might increase. This has happened in Algeria, North Africa. During the 1990s the Armed Islamic Group (GIA) killed thousands of people in schools, universities and cities, in its war against the Algerian dictatorship government. In response, the Algerian security forces are responsible for the killings, torture and disappearances of thousands of Algerians.

Terrorism and the media

Terrorism is dramatic and horrifying. The media (television, radio and Internet) brings attention to a terrorist's cause. Terrorists also set out deliberately to frighten the audience. They want them to believe that if they, or their government, do not behave in a certain way they can expect more terrifying violence.

Terrorism is therefore about making gruesome attacks in as spectacular a manner possible. Israel's former Prime Minister Benjamin Netanyahu believes that if the media were to give less attention to terrorism, then it would decrease. This is because its prime purpose, to win attention, would fail.

The media has been accused of interfering harmfully during terrorist incidents. In 1985, a passenger jet was **hijacked** and landed in Beirut, Lebanon, by Hizbullah, an **Islamic extremist** Lebanese group fighting Israel. As days passed, emotional life stories of 39 US hostages were broadcast across television networks. The public in the USA became so upset on behalf of the hostages that US President Reagan was forced to give in to Hizbullah's requests and ask Israel to release over 700 prisoners, some of whom had committed acts of terrorism.

A hijacker armed with an AK-47 rifle looks out from the hijacked TWA flight 867 at Beirut International Airport in Lebanon, June 1985.

4339

Parts of the media have also been criticized for not calling those who commit terrorism, 'terrorists'. 'HonestReporting.com', a media campaign group, has criticized news agencies such as the BBC World Service, Reuters and MSNBC.com for refusing to describe **suicide bombers** as 'terrorists'. Instead, news organizations often use words like 'militants', 'commandos' or 'activists'. Some journalists believe it is not their job to make judgements about whether an armed attack has been carried out by a 'terrorist' or a 'freedom fighter'. Rather it is their job to report events and explain to the world why particular terrorist attacks occur.

Increasing our fear

Television images and volumes of newspaper articles have increased our fear of terrorism, especially after live coverage of hijacked passenger jets crashing into the World Trade Center on 11 September 2001. Sometimes footage is so frightening that all of us become victims, perhaps experiencing depression or fear that we are in danger or under threat all the time. But it is worth remembering that less than one in a hundred thousand people experience an aircraft hijacking, and most hijackings end safely.

Journalists run for protection as armed clashes break out between Israel's army and Palestinian fighters at Lion's Gate, Old City, Jerusalem.

Terrorism and you

One way to become more involved in studying terrorism is to choose a particular incident and follow the way the incident is reported in the newspapers over the following days. Notice how some news reporters might refer to the incident as 'terrorism', while others might say an 'attack' occurred. Read about the tactics used by the terrorists. Who are the suspects? Who seem to be the intended victims?

The Internet is also a vast source of information about terrorism. Many websites such as the BBC online (www.bbc.co.uk), CNN online (www.cnn.com) and TerrorismAnswers.com have a wide range of articles and facts on terrorism. The Internet also presents the chance to look at a particular terrorist attack and notice the different responses to it in different parts of the world.

For example, *Al-Ahram* is a respected newspaper in Egypt – a country made up of mainly Arab Muslims. Many people in this region of the world view Israel (a Jewish-run nation) as acting illegally and violently in stopping Palestinians (also mainly Muslim) owning their own country. In 2002, anti-Israel activists bombed an Israeli hotel and fired a missile at an Israeli passenger jet in Kenya. One of *Al-Ahram's* reporters in Egypt described the incidents as 'daring attacks on Israeli interests'. While one of Israel's main papers, the *Jerusalem Post*, strongly condemned the incidents where eleven people died as 'terrorist attacks'.

"Solutions start at home, with you and me."

Charles Secrett, Director, Friends of the Earth UK

These women are among thousands of people protesting on the streets of London in October 2001. Even though many people disagree with governments, most do not see the need to commit violence against other members of the public.

Try looking at political violence in other parts of the world, such as Colombia, Ireland, India and Pakistan. What are the different responses of politicians and the newspaper reporters? Why might these differences occur?

Another way to develop your knowledge of terrorism is by contacting politicians and government departments. Write or send an email, perhaps asking what is being done to prevent terrorism at home or abroad. Look at government websites, and find out which countries travellers are warned not to visit. Ask why people are advised not to travel there. Is the government being too cautious? Or does our government not warn us enough? Write to them and let them know your views.

Facts and figures

Terror groups

Al-Qaida (The Base)
Islamic extremist group, headed by Osama bin Laden, last known to be based in Afghanistan. Aims to spread worldwide holy war against US and **Western** interests.

Black September
Palestinian Islamic extremist group, established in 1970. Used aircraft **hijackings,** kidnappings and assassinations, waging war against Israel.

ETA (Euskadi ta Askatasuna)
Separatist group whose goal is a separate homeland for Spain's and France's Basque population. They are responsible for around 800 deaths since 1968.

FARC (Revolutionary Armed Forces of Colombia)
Extreme **left-wing** group that aims to protect rural peasants by conducting **guerrilla** warfare against **right-wing** government forces.

GIA (Armed Islamic Group)
Islamic extremist group based in Algeria. Seeks to overthrow the secular (non-religious) Algerian FLN government.

Hamas
'Islamic Resistance Movement' based in Gaza and West Bank of Israel. Wages a holy war to free Palestine from Israel's rule.

Hizbullah
Islamic extremist group based in Lebanon. Its goal is to establish Islamic rule in Lebanon and to free all Arab lands from occupation by non-Muslims.

Islamic Jihad
Islamic extremist group, which aims to establish an Islamic Palestinian state and destroy Israel.

JRA (Japanese Red Army)
Small, left-wing international terror group, which aims to overthrow the Japanese government and bring about a worldwide revolution.

Jemaa Islamiya
'Islamic Association', Islamic extremist group, aiming for a single Islamic state including Indonesia, Malaysia and Singapore.

November 17

Extreme left-wing Greek group, whose name honours a student demonstration against the Greek dictatorship government on 17 November 1973. Carried out 21 murders between 1975 and 2000, before a small number of group leaders were caught in 2001. Now thought to be inactive.

PKK (Kurdistan Workers Party)

Left-wing, separatist group based in Turkey. Aims for a separate state for 15 million Kurds in southeast Turkey. PKK attacks in Turkey have killed over 8500 people – almost half were ordinary members of the public, the majority Kurds. Currently under **ceasefire**.

Provisional IRA (Provisional Irish Republican Army)

Separatist group based in Northern Ireland. Aims to unite Northern Ireland with the Irish Republic, thus ending rule by the UK. Currently under ceasefire.

Real IRA (Real Irish Republican Army)

Group formed in 1997 from within the Provisional IRA. Opposed the Provisional IRA's ceasefire policy in the late 1990s, vowing to continue armed struggle against Britain.

Red Army Faction (Rote Armee Fraktion)

Extreme left-wing guerrilla group active in West Germany from 1968 (popularly known as the Baader-Meinhof gang, after its leading members Andreas Baader and Ulrike Meinhof, who were arrested in 1972).

Red Brigades (Brigate Rosse)

Extreme left-wing guerrilla groups active in Italy during the 1970s and 1980s.

Shining Path (Sendero Luminoso)

Extreme left-wing guerrilla group in Peru, formed in 1980 to overthrow the government and fight for the interests of the rural poor.

Tamil Tigers (The Liberation Tigers of Tamil Eelam, LTTE)

Separatist group seeking an independent state in Sri Lanka for **ethnic** Tamils. They have been under a ceasefire since December 2001.

Further information

Contacts

Centre for the Study of Terrorism and Political Violence
Offers university courses and advice on terrorism.
University of St Andrews
St Andrews, Fife KY16 9AL
UK
Tel: 01334 476161
email: cstpv@st-andrews.ac.uk
www.standrews.ac.uk/academic/intrel/ research/cstpv/index.html

Federation of American Scientists
Easy-to-use guide on future terrorism and US war on terrorism.
1717 K Street NW, Suite 209
Washington DC 20036
USA
email: fas@fas.org
www.fas.org/terrorism/index.html

National Organization for Women (NOW)
Campaigns to stop violence against women.
Can be contacted at their website at:
www.now.org/

The Nuclear Control Institute
Clear advice and information on nuclear terrorism.
1000 Connecticut Avenue
Suite 410
Washington DC 20036
USA
email: nci@nci.org
www.nci.org/

The Internet

Council for Foreign Relations in cooperation with The Markle Foundation
terrorismanswers.com
Clear and excellent online information about violent groups, tactics, incidents and motives.

The Terrorism Research Center
– experts from Australia, the USA, UK
www.terrorism.com/
Daily news analysis, incidents calendar and many links.

US State Department Patterns of Global Terrorism 2001
www.state.gov/s/ct/rls/pgtrpt/2001/
Covers all terror groups around the world and details 11 September 2001 attacks and the world's response.

Further reading

Terrorism: Understanding the Global Threat,
David J. Whittaker (Pearson Education,
2002)
Easy-to-use explanation of disputes driving
terror groups.

Inside Terrorism, Bruce Hoffman (Victor
Gollancz, 1998)
In-depth study of terrorism from the world's
leading expert.

The New Jackals, Simon Reeve (Andre
Deutsch, 1999)
Following the life of Razi Yousef, one of the
world's most vicious terrorists.

Glossary

anthrax
biological weapons agent that causes illness or death

biological weapon
disease-causing organism used as a weapon to injure or kill (such as ricin, smallpox or anthrax germs)

ceasefire
declaration by a terrorist group that it is stopping violence

chemical nerve agent
poison that if refined can destroy a human's central nervous system (such as sarin gas, VX droplets or gas, and tabun droplets or gas)

Christian crusaders
Christian soldiers from Europe sent mainly during the 11th and 12th centuries to recover Jerusalem and the surrounding Holy Land from the control of Muslims

civilian
person who is not in the armed forces (army, navy, air force) or the police

counter-terrorism
ways to detect, prevent and stop terrorism

cult
religious group with extreme sense of worship, often directed towards a particular figure or object

democratic
supporting a form of government in which the people have the right to elect the government

diplomacy/diplomatic
how countries talk and deal with one another

embassy
country's official headquarters abroad, headed by an ambassador

ethnic
of a particular race or tribe of people

extremism
promotion or support of very extreme or harsh measures

fanatic
person who holds excessive enthusiasm for a cause, possibly willing to die for it

guerrilla
person (non-state activist) who uses warfare and other terrorist methods to bring about political change

hacker
person who uses a computer to gain unauthorized access to data and computer systems

hijack
seize control illegally of (an aeroplane, ship or vehicle)

human rights abuses
failure to give people their basic human rights (such as freedom from cruelty and torture)

hunger strike
refusal to eat until a set of conditions are met

ideological
to do with a set of political ideals, such as Marxism or Fascism

independence movement
group or set of groups seeking freedom or self-government for their homeland

Islamic extremists
extremist followers of the Islamic religion (Muslims) believing in harsh measures against their identified enemies

left-wing
to do with beliefs that national resources and wealth should be more evenly shared among all the people

liberation
freedom

martyr
person who is killed because of, or dies for the sake of, their political or religious beliefs

Marxism/socialism
communist ideas (extreme left-wing) put forward by Karl Marx and others who said the community should own the means of production (such as farms, businesses, power plants) rather than small groups of business persons or elites

Middle East
countries near to where Europe meets Asia, running from Egypt in the west to Afghanistan in the east – including Iran, Iraq, Saudi Arabia and Turkey

non-state group
unofficial group, not controlled by government or army

occupying forces
army holding possession of a territory that is historically not theirs

Palestinian Liberation Organization (PLO)
Arab organization founded in 1964 to bring about an independent state of Palestine

political idealism
strong belief in a set of political ideals, about how the community, country or wider world should be run

radioactivity
spread of harmful atomic particles

revolutionaries
people seeking to overthrow a government

right-wing
strong ideas that government should not interfere in people's lives – supporters of right-wing politics are opposed to left-wing ideas such as socialism and Marxism

separatist
person who wishes their people or country to be separate from a nation or occupying force

Soviet Union
empire that existed 1922–91, with Russia dominating surrounding republics

suicide bomber
person who dies when delivering a bomb to its target

United Nations (UN)
international organization of 191 countries based in New York, USA, which works to promote peace, security and humanitarian policies

weapons of mass destruction (WMD)
weapons that contain chemical, biological or nuclear agents, which could possibly cause many thousands or millions of deaths

West/Western
Christian and democratic countries, usually the USA, Europe and Australasia

Index

Titles in the *Just the Facts* series include:

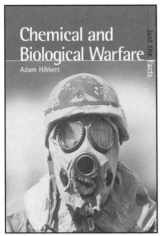

Hardback   0 431 16160 7

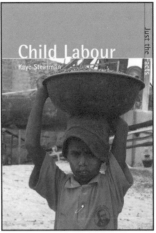

Hardback   0 431 16161 5

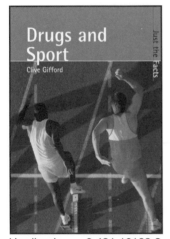

Hardback   0 431 16162 3

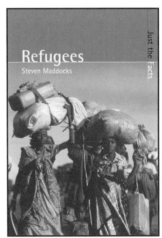

Hardback   0 431 16163 1

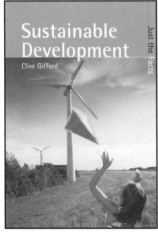

Hardback   0 431 16164 X

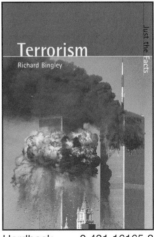

Hardback   0 431 16165 8

Find out about the other titles in this series on our website www.heinemann.co.uk/library